COA10-26-11

◄NOTES►

◀TEN QUESTIONS▶

The Insider's Guide To Saving Money On Auto Insurance

HIDDEN DISCOUNTS REVEALED

By John David

Drawings by Sarah David

◄TABLE OF CONTENTS►

◀INTRODUCTION▶

For over 24 months, I sold auto insurance and other Property and Casualty (P&C) insurance products for a major online-based carrier selling in more than 29 states. For 15 consecutive months, I was the #1 ranked Sales Agent in the nation for that company. The benefit of my experience is what I am offering you now.

The most effective way to use this guide is to own both the ebook and paperback versions. The ebook offers convenience and portability, which means you will actually be able to read it on your breaks, and whenever you have a spare moment. You can then later refer to the paperback, where you will have the ability to take notes, make highlights, add tabs, <u>and underline the important concepts and discounts most relevant to you.</u>

If you already own a previous ebook version of *Ten Questions*, simply remove and reload it to your library to obtain the current edition, which has been updated to version 1.1, optimized, and reformatted especially for ebook readers. "Lending" is enabled.

You can switch insurance carriers any time you want, as often as you want. You do not have to wait until your current policy renews in order to do so. Younger drivers may find this strategy to be the most cost-effective. If you will be switching mid-term, make sure to ask about any cancellation fees, and do the math if there is a fee. If it costs you $25 to save $200, then that is an obvious no-brainer.

▪DISCLOSURE▪

This material is presented for informational purposes only, and does not represent a recommendation of any particular course of action. **Consult an attorney for legal advice, as absolutely none is contained within the following text.** You understand that by reading beyond this introduction you accept and agree that your decisions remain your own, and not those of this author, or the publisher of this material. **If you disagree with this disclosure**, please stop reading now.

▪DISCLAIMER▪

Every state has different requirements for auto insurance, and different underwriting factors, and they are constantly changing. Therefore, **it is the responsibility of the reader** to become informed about the particular factors affecting auto insurance rates in their state, and to act on them accordingly. Both the author and publisher disclaim any responsibility for the decisions that you make regarding your auto insurance coverage.

◀THE GUIDE▶

The title of this book is "**Ten Questions**," and I chose that name because within those ten questions are thousands of your dollars in insurance premiums. When you get a quote for your auto insurance, you will be asked about your living situation, driving history, accident reports, and other factors. **How you answer those questions determines the amount of "risk" that you represent, versus the amount of "premium" that you will pay.** Risk premium is negated by discount, and that means the more discounts you receive from your "base rate,"* the lower your premiums.

Your base rate is also determined through the responses to the questions that you will be asked. This is referred to as "tiering"* for risk, but it acts like a discount, so we will consider it to be one. **This guide will reveal to you the "correct" answers to those ten questions, and it will immediately save you money.** That is why you should study it carefully before you start or renew your auto insurance policy. Keep it as a reference for every time your policy renews, and be sure to update your coverages and discounts as your family circumstances change.

A note here: While you read, you will see many "technical" or trade-type terminologies. These will be marked with an asterisk, (*) and all of these terms are referenced and explained in the appendix. **Most of them are just fancy words for simple things, anyway.**

Each state has decided what rating factors, discounts, and fees may be used, and which may not. Insurance companies do not *determine* these factors, as is commonly believed, but they in fact *respond* to them. Once a discount is allowed, it will soon be offered. If a fee is allowed, most likely it will be charged. It is the same with many rate tiering factors, such as the much despised "credit-based insurance score." **This and other factors affect the total risk assessment, or "underwriting" that you represent to an insurance company.**

How to use this book:

If you need to purchase or renew your auto insurance policy now or very soon, then this is the guide for you. In a rush? Skip directly to "Sample Quote Process," (page 41) which is an example of the quoting, rating, and discounting process from start to finish. If you do this, remember that you may have to thumb to the appendix once or twice, **since you will see terms that you may not have seen before.** Tab the appendix if you are reading this in paper form.

Think about those ten questions, and how they apply to you. Remember which answers generate the most "discounts," and therefore the lowest possible rate for you. Each one is discussed and examples are given. All of these examples are based on my real world experience, and the thousands of policies I have written. Remember that you do not have to wait until your policy "renews" or "expires," to switch carriers and take advantage of lower rates with better coverages. **You can do it tomorrow if you like.**

Each of those questions is referenced in at least one of three chapters, making it easy to find additional information on a specific one, and each chapter is cross-referenced when needed, to make referring back and forth very simple.

If you have, or will soon have young drivers in your household, you will find the section on "Youthful Driver Strategies" (page 3) very helpful. **If you consider yourself an "advanced" auto insurance consumer, with above-average knowledge**, you will want to pay special attention to the section on "Advanced Topics," (page 46). Most of the information found there will not be relevant to many readers, at least until after you have studied this guide.

When you have finished reading *Ten Questions*, you will know more about auto insurance than most agents do. Best of all, you will be prepared to answer those ten questions with *your* best interests at heart, and those of your family. By the way, thanks for hanging on and finishing the introduction. **If you benefit from the guide, tell your friends and family about it, and lend them your ebook. They will thank you for it!**

◄CHAPTER ONE►

RISK

"Risk" is what you are transferring from yourself to your insurance company when you buy any type of insurance policy. **Automobile policies primarily involve the risk of liability that is potentially incurred by damaging another person or their property.** The more risk, or likelihood of a claim, the more premium associated with that risk. A driver with three at-fault accidents in the last three years, or even three "not-at-fault" accidents, is certainly a higher risk than a driver with a spotless claims and driving record.

Your goal as a consumer of auto insurance products is to minimize the amount of risk that you are seen to represent, and this is directly related to the "rating tier" (and therefore discount) that you will receive.

Tiering and rating factors vary from one company to another, and include such things as the obvious ones like age, credit history, and driving record. Not so obvious are factors like military status, occupation, and the duration of time you have been with a particular company. The number of factors used to "tier" a driver can be as few as ten with some of the major online carriers, **to as many as several million with the "membership based" underwriters.** (Those that require you to "join" them in order be become insured).

If you qualify for "membership" with one of these companies, you will over time most likely see your rates improve, even if only incrementally, because having more rating factors can mean more "discounts" for you. In general, if you are older and more established, with a stable job, insurance, and credit history, you will most likely be better off with a company that uses many factors. If you are younger and less established, you may be better off with a company that only uses a few. <u>The key here is to recognize the point that you are no longer improving your "tier" with your company, because that is your cue to start shopping your coverage to a more "complicated" underwriter.</u>

▪Your garaging address, for example, is a primary rating factor for risk▪

Two adjacent zip codes, literally across the street from each other may be 10%, 20%, 30% or more different in price. **Keep this in mind when you pick out your next home or apartment.** If you are considering two or three properties to buy or rent, <u>remember to</u>

quote your insurance from each zip code (if any difference) to see how much more or less each will cost you. A two minute drive that saves you 30% on your auto insurance may be one of the best investments you ever make.

"Are there any other drivers in your household? Are they relatives or roommates? Would anyone else but you drive your vehicle?"

These questions are used to determine who, other than the "Primary Named Insured," or PNI,* might possibly be driving the vehicles on the policy. **Insurance companies definitely want to collect the premium dollars due for the 16 year-old in the household**, especially if she might be driving her grandmother's Cadillac. When allowed, most companies will require you to add or exclude all other licensed drivers in your household, especially if they are related to you.

▪The most important concept to understand about those "other driver" questions is simply this▪

In most every state, if there are other drivers in your household **who are not related to you**, and they have their own vehicle and insurance, **then you are not required to cover them on your policy, even in the strictest "limited exclusion"** state. This is a not an issue in states that allow a flat driver exclusion,* since most likely you will want high risk drivers off of your policy (and out of your drivers' seat) anyway, and what better excuse for that than "sorry, my insurance won't cover you."

This one crucial factor may be the most important to you when tiering your policy for the risk you represent:

If a driver does not need or want to be on your policy, exclude them if exclusions are available in your state. You may be charged a fee for doing so, usually not more than $25, no matter how many drivers in your household that you will be excluding. If they are actually not going to be driving your vehicle, obviously you do not want to pay premium as if they were, **so the key here is to exclude them.**

This gets tricky in some states, though, (New York and New Jersey, for example) where exclusions, especially for spouses, are simply not allowed. Again, if the other drivers have their own vehicles and insurance, and do not drive your vehicle, **(or have never been licensed in any state)**, and you can provide "verification"* of these facts, **you can avoid having unwanted drivers added to your policy in the first place.** This may apply even in the stricter limited exclusion states.

Be sure to ask if exclusions are available if you are always being told that "you have to insure all the drivers in the household on your policy, even if they don't drive your car." Agents will tell you this to avoid writing the policy with the exclusions, for fear that you will be allowing the drivers to operate the vehicle anyway, and they will be subjecting their company to uncompensated "risk."

▪Youthful Driver Strategies▪

Adding a young driver to your policy can be one of the most fear-inducing experiences a parent can know, both because of the amount of increased premium involved, and the idea of setting the youngster loose on the freeways of the world. Once the young driver obtains a "learner's permit," they are typically covered under your policy as a "permitted driver," without any additional premium charge. Keep them permitted on your policy for as long as possible, both because it is usually free, and because they will gain valuable driving experience.

Once they become a "licensed" operator, (and they will push for this as quickly as possible) you must add them to the policy as such. Your premium will increase substantially, usually between $70 and $300 per month, depending on the discounts you (and they) receive, and the type of vehicles/coverages on the policy. Often it is just as expensive to add a cheap vehicle to the policy with the new driver, as it is to add the driver alone. If this is feasible for you, you will benefit because they will not be driving your nice, expensive, clean car around, and also because you can carry "liability only" on the cheaper car. In the event of an at-fault occurrence, simply walk away from the car and get another, instead of bothering with pricy repairs.

"Accident Forgiveness" can be a very valuable coverage to have on your policy at this point, for obvious reasons (see "Coverages," page 36) so make sure you have it, if available, even if you have to pay for it.

Often, folks will call in to add the young driver to their policy as a permitted operator, then "forget" to notify their insurance carrier when the child becomes licensed. This may lead to the denial of a claim, because most insurance contracts contain language that clearly specifies that you must add them to your policy when you are required to do so. **If you do not, you may have issues with claims being denied, or with the after-the-fact assessment of additional premium, all the way back to when the child first became licensed.**

Make sure your child completes the driver's training course, and if offered, the defensive driving course as well. These two discounts, along with the good student discount, can save you as much as $200 or more each policy term. (See "Discounts," page 19). **Insurance companies typically use a process call "Additional Driver Discovery," which is essentially a third-party service that scours driver's license databases and cross-references them with addresses, to discover additional licensed operators living at your address, in your household.** They especially focus on "Youthful Driver Discovery," which is finding out about Junior and his freshly minted license, and requiring you to either add or exclude him from your policy.

If you do not want your child to be added to your policy, either because you don't think they deserve to drive, you can't afford it, or whatever, then do not allow them to become licensed in the first place. Do not sign off on the license. Once they have a license, if you want to avoid paying premium for them, you will have to complete a named, or "flat" driver exclusion form, if available in your state. Another option is returning ("surrendering") the child's license to the local DMV, and submitting verification to your insurance carrier that you have done so.

If you have a shared custody situation, and the child is already insured by the other parent, you will not have to add them to your policy, as long as you can provide verification of this coverage.

Keep in mind that adding young drivers to your policy increases your liability exposure tremendously, and you will want your policy limits to reflect that. (See "**Umbrella Policies**" under "Advanced Topics" page 46).

"Will you be using the vehicle for any business or commercial purpose?"

This is very much a red flag for potential liability, because the business use of a vehicle increases the liability exposure tremendously, and many companies will not write a policy with this kind of risk at all, or will surcharge* such an exorbitant amount that no reasonable person would buy the policy from them anyway. You may be asked a series of questions about the use of your vehicle if you disclose a business use. **Some companies and agents will instantly "DNQ"* (does not qualify) you if you disclose commercial use.** This means that they cannot and will not sell you an insurance policy.

▪Remember this▪

Driving yourself to work is not a business use. Taking care of your business with your car is not a business use. **Delivering pizzas or newspapers with your car is a business use,** so keep in mind that the undeclared commercial use of a vehicle can and may result in the denial of any potential claim, or the after-the-fact assessment of additional premium. If you use your vehicle commercially, you should insure it as such.

But too often people will reply, when asked this question in one of its many variations, "sure, I take care of my business with my car." What the question really means is simply "do you operate a business using the vehicle?" **Even if you are reimbursed for your mileage by your company, simply driving yourself to and from work in your vehicle is not** *necessarily* **a business use, so avoid this surcharge when legitimately possible.**

Keep in mind, though, that if you are a salesperson, real estate agent/broker, or a property manager, for example, you may still be better off with a "personal lines" insurance policy, as opposed to a "commercial" liability policy, even if you do end up paying a surcharge. **Ideally, you always want to avoid paying for coverages that you do not need or could not ever possibly use,** and while commercial policies make sense under certain circumstances, there are many other cases where that extra premium could be better spent elsewhere. Make sure to discuss your business use with a trusted agent or financial advisor, and if a commercial policy is warranted, by all means get one.

"Will you commute to a workplace in New York (NY) or New Jersey (NJ)?"

This question would never be asked of you if you live in California (CA), for example, but if you live in a state adjacent to NY or NJ, and you "commute" to those states, you may well be surcharged, **because your insurance company must match the coverage of the state the vehicle is being driven in, if and while it is being driven in that state.** Keep this in mind when answering this question:

Merely driving into those states occasionally to shop or visit relatives is not "commuting" by any definition.

"How many miles per day/week/year will you be driving your vehicle?"

In the states that use this risk factor, total miles driven per year will strongly affect your premium, sometimes doubling or tripling the base rate. **The more miles, the more premium.** You are allowed to "self-report" the answer to this question, and it will seldom be verified unless extremely low annual mileage is claimed. **This particular factor is discussed further in the "discounts" section.**

Some companies are now offering a telemetry based discount, whereby in exchange for installing a GPS-based tracking device in your car, you get (or may possibly get!) this discount. If you don't mind your movements being tracked 24/7 by your insurance company, you might consider this discount.

"How is your driving record? Do you have any accidents, violations, or claims in the last three years? Any major violations in the last five?"

Different companies will rate on violations and accidents differently. I cannot stress this enough. One company may not offer coverage at all to anyone who has a DUI. Some count major violations for five years (like DUI), some for three. The point being that it is possible to minimize your rates, even if you have serious issues with your driving record, by shopping your exact record and matching it to a company that offers underwriting that favors you.

Step one in this process is easy if you have a perfect driving record—the answers to these questions are always simply "no." If you are not certain, the easiest way to find out exactly what is on your driving records is simply to order a motor vehicle report (MVR)* from your local DMV. You may be charged a nominal fee, but it will certainly be worth that small cost, because when it comes to this area, knowledge is both power and money. Knowing your exact driving history and accident report is crucial, because of the "discovery truth indicator" that will lower your tier, as explained in the next section.

▪Discovery Truth Indicator▪

Also known as "liar liar, pants on fire," this is a re-tiering that is applied to you if information is found on the underwriting reports that contradicts what you have disclosed. In other words, failing to disclose accidents and violations will result in higher premiums when the occurrences are "discovered" during the underwriting process.

Many people who are not aware of this will call in and say, "just run my reports, you'll find everything." However, simply not disclosing the correct information will definitely cost you extra premium. Your strategy here is to avoid this at all costs, by obtaining a copy of your MVR and accident history before you quote your policy.

This "failure to disclose" penalty can be as much as 15% or more, and it is highly controversial, even among agents. **It can penalize decent people who legitimately were unsure of whether that ticket for speeding was 2 years and 10 months ago, or 3 years and 2 months.**

Listing the ticket will usually result in the driver being rated for it, **whether or not it comes up on the reports,** the logic being that, "they know something the system doesn't know," or some such nonsense. If their records are clear, then I have just surcharged them by 10% or more. **If I don't list it, and it is on the reports, I will have caused a rate increase of 15% or more. A no-win situation, in either case.**

On the bright side, if this happens to you with one company (your rate suddenly increases substantially when quoting) ask the agent why, or look deeper into the quote program where it will explain why this occurred. ("You told us this, we found that"). If possible, ask the agent to tell you exactly what was found on the accident and MVR reports, including dates and amounts of claims, **then take this knowledge to another company for a quote, where you will not be charged this penalty.**

◄CHAPTER TWO►

DISCOUNTS

Discounts are obviously "where the money is at," or isn't, in this case. **They are the money that you put back into your pocket after your rate is determined.** When you ask an agent to generate a rate quote for you, the agent will provide you with a number that already includes the discounts that agent has found for you based on the answers you gave to the "ten questions." You may not have answered the questions the most effectively, **and the agent may not have known or cared to offer you all the discounts that were available.** Your job is to make sure that neither of these things happens.

▪The perfect strategy for you to follow as a consumer of auto insurance products is to "stack" as many discounts on top of each other as you possibly can▪

My intention is not to deter anyone from working with an agent, although it is certainly not necessary to do so, especially once you have finished reading this guide. There are many reputable online-based companies that you may deal with, and you will never have to speak to an actual agent, should you choose not to.

However, at some point you may be asked to provide "verification"* of this thing or that. If so, you either can verify your eligibility for the particular discount, or you cannot. Even should you "lose" a particular discount because you could not "verify" it, you certainly had nothing to lose by claiming it.

Another little-known but very important fact in the auto insurance business:

▪Few if any of the discounts you claim will ever verified by anyone▪

But do be prepared to provide verification if needed. As with any discount that you lose because you could not verify it, consider this a teaching opportunity, and a reason to shop your insurance even harder at the next renewal.

Most everything said on the phone to an agent is recorded, (remember that you are being recorded as well!) and agents are scored on how well they question and correctly rate you the caller and potential policy holder. A lousy job by the agent results in a bad risk that is incorrectly priced for the company. A perfect job by the agent? A properly written and accurately priced policy that stays on the books and renews endlessly with zero claims.

If you talk to an agent, make sure that they have the time to work with you, and an interest in doing so. Show some respect for them and their specialized knowledge, and they will become your confidante and advocate. Why would you do this? **Because agents get paid for selling you a policy, usually whether or not it is a good policy, or a bad one.** They know the number one factor for many potential policy holders is very simply the price of the insurance. Use this to your advantage, let the agent be your friend, and you will both win.

"Online" companies allow you to "be your own agent," by rating yourself and finding your own discounts online. When you complete the quoting process online and bind* your own coverage, that is effectively what you are doing. Keep in mind that much of the information you enter into the program will be electronically verified immediately, resulting in potential red flags for underwriters, like incorrect addresses, or zip codes that don't match driver's licenses, and so forth. If you will be quoting yourself online without an agent, make sure you have all your relevant information at hand, and enter everything as accurately as possible to avoid extra scrutiny of your policy.

▪Three major reports are used to rate you in most states, (accident, driving, and credit) with one major exception▪

The Credit Based Insurance Score, or CBIS,* is not used in a few key states, of these, California is the largest and most relevant market.

▪CBIS is perhaps the most important discount of all when it is used, and where allowed, we are told that 92% of all insurance companies use it▪

You will see, or be read a disclosure, then asked for your Social Security Number (SSN). This is a sure sign than it will most likely be used. Many people dislike the use of this score, and often unnecessarily so, as it usually helps them more than it hurts them. In a perfect world, paying bills late would not be an indicator of potential claims incidence. We are told that it is. Therefore over time, obviously the higher your CBIS, the better rates you will get. However, in one succinct statement, what follows is the *most* important issue to understand about the CBIS:

▪It is only used to rate ("tier") on one driver, the first one listed, even if there are several other drivers on the same policy▪

Since you will be driving for at least the next 10, 20, or 50 years, and you will be buying auto insurance for most if not all of those years, **your goal should be to continuously reduce your total premiums paid, by maximizing your underwriting rating factors and discounts.** CBIS is not a flat out FICO (credit score) number times a multiplier of some kind. It is based on many factors, sometimes 12 or more, and it varies by state. The nuances of each state are not really important, but what is important to remember is this:

▪**Two different people, usually a husband and wife, (this is the most commonly seen example of this) may have vastly different factors, and subsequently a rating difference of two tiers or more between them**▪

Obviously you want the driver on the policy with the best CBIS score to be the "primary named insured" or PNI.* If your CBIS is stellar, you want that to be you.

To easily determine this factor, regardless of what state you live in, simply quote the policy from both perspectives, first with one spouse (or driver) as PNI, then the other. **Make sure that the coverages you request are *absolutely* identical.** Do this from different IP addresses, for example, do one quote by the husband at home, one quote by the wife at the office.

Some programs will link quotes from the same IP address and "capture" the data from both, resulting in identical or nearly so rates. **I know that my system would do so if I generated the quotes, so asking an agent to do this for you is typically useless.**

CBIS is only one rating factor among many, but it is a great place to start saving money on your auto insurance. **Your strategy here is to always know who has the best CBIS among all the drivers that will be on the policy, and to always list that driver first.**

▪Homeowner versus Renter rating factors▪

"Do you own or rent your home?"

For some reason, a household that pays "rent" to a bank each month, (since very few people actually "own" their home, "free and clear") is somehow a better risk than one that pays rent to a landlord, who then makes a "payment" to that same bank. **The "homeowners" discount will be substantial when offered, as much as ten percent or more.**

Some companies offer additional options to obfuscate this, **or to offer certain people less discount.** These will appear as "live with parents," or "own *mobile* home." Watch out for this question. <u>Determine whether or not you "own" your home.</u> If you do, be sure to claim this discount.

▪Teaser, or "switchover" discount▪

This is the most often overlooked discount. Nearly every company will offer you a first term or "teaser" rate that includes an "internet" or "online" discount, and may also include an "existing coverage," or "switchover" discount to help pay for any cancellation fees you may have for changing insurers. <u>Those "cancellation" fees are almost never allowed at renewal, so when you are ready to shop your rates, just make sure you request a "non-renewal"* of your policy, not a "cancellation,"* and you will never pay any of these fees.</u>

You will get these teaser discounts every term if you are willing to switch companies each term. **These two discounts are usually 5% each, so find a company offering both, and that's another 10% off your rate.** Of course, the loss of this first-term discount at renewal is no reason to immediately jump ship to another company, but it is a reason to shop around if your rate mysteriously goes up 5% every renewal from the company you are with now.

▪Prior insurance discount, duration, and amount▪

"Do you have insurance now? If so, how long have you had insurance? What are the limits of that policy?

This line of questioning is used to determine your "proof of insurance" or POI*. Prior insurance is considered a strong rating factor, and coming into a new policy with high limits lowers your perceived risk to the underwriter.

▪Keep in mind though, that any POI you claim will always be verified to some extent, or you should always count on the fact that it will be▪

This means that you always want the answers to this line of questioning to be "yes, I have liability insurance now. I've had it for a long time, and I have lots of it."

"Amount" of POI is rated up to the magical number at which the discount is maxed out, which is typically "100k/300k."* (This means 100 thousand dollars per person/300 thousand per accident). A few "preferred" companies may offer slightly greater discounts for having even higher limits, like 300k/500k. **The interesting thing about this question is that it is not asked as, "how long have you carried this limit?" but "how much do you have right now?"** The fact that you called or went online with your existing carrier *two days ago* and increased all your limits to that sweet spot, is irrelevant to the question that is being asked today.

▪Some important things to remember about POI▪

Commercial insurance policies usually do not count, although if you were covered under a business policy while you drove a company car, this may qualify. **Being a "named insured" on someone else's policy does count, even if for only one day.** Having had "foreign" auto insurance (anywhere outside of the U.S.) does not count, **although Canadian polices usually do.**

If you have lapsed your coverage for 24 hours or less, most companies will offer you a "grace period" and will rate you as if you still had continuous POI. You must bind your new policy within that first 24 hours. If you miss that deadline, some companies will still give you a partial discount for having had coverage within the last 30 days.

With that in mind, the agent (or company) may immediately ask you, "can you verify your current POI?"

Providing verification will be as simple as printing out a copy of your declarations page from your current policy, and sending it in by fax or email. The POI rating factor for "duration" or "how *long* have you had coverage?" is typically rated up to six years (the longer, the better) **but in most cases only the first six months or year is "verified" through submission of documents.**

There is a military "exemption" to this POI requirement, where if you can document deployment, had insurance before deployment, and obtain new insurance within 30 days of your return, you can be rated for no lapse of coverage. **Be sure to ask about this if you believe you qualify. If you do, it will be a very strong discount for you.**

If you are a young or new driver, just starting out with your own insurance history, consider asking a friend or relative to add you (temporarily) to their "high-limit" policy (100k/300k or better) immediately before you begin to quote your own insurance. Your answers to the POI questions will then correctly be "less than one year," and "100k/300k," and your rates will be much better than if you had not followed this strategy.

In New York the price difference for this rating factor alone is huge, and may be the one discount that allows you to afford your own insurance in the first place! You would also get the "switchover" discount if it is available. Even if the term of your "prior insurance" is as little as one day, you will still get the discount for having it.

Proper use of the POI discount will usually ensure that you get much higher limits of coverage for the same cost as "minimum liability," if nothing else. The exception to this would be that if you have a history of claims, you will still be asked to pay more for better coverage, because you are a bigger risk. If this is happening to you, you need to clean up your driving record a little bit before you can expect the best possible rates from anyone.

▪Driver experience or "duration" discount▪

"How old were you when you got your driver's license in the United States?"

This is *the* critical discount factor for young drivers, East Coast drivers, and drivers new to this country. Often drivers in states with good public transit may be in their 30's or older when they are first licensed. Rates can double or triple on this one factor alone. Many people still believe in some mystical threshold for "driving age" discounts, and most think that it is 25 years old.

What is more commonly used as a rating factor is the amount of time since the driver was first licensed in the US, until now. The more the better. A 24 year-old first licensed at age 15 has nine years of driving experience. A 25 year-old first licensed at age 24 has one year of driving experience. Who should get the better rate? Of course the driver with nine years of driving experience.

Likewise it is with foreign drivers, newly licensed in this country. Even though you were licensed in your country at age 12, and have been driving on the "wrong" side of the road for 20 years, you still have little or no "driving experience" for rating purposes. When you are quoting your U.S. auto insurance policy, and say that you were first licensed here *last year*, your rate will most certainly be high, with any carrier.

▪The major exception here is that Canadian driving experience is usually an acceptable substitute▪

Keep in mind that most of the information you give in response to this question is merely self-reported, **and will not be verified in any meaningful way beyond determining that you do in fact have a valid license.** Theoretically, I suppose it could be, by requiring every policy holder to provide abstracts from every license they have ever held in every state, but that's not likely to happen.

▪Mileage Discount▪

"How many miles per week or year will you be driving the vehicle?"

Another discount related to "driver experience," is the "usage," or "mileage driven" rating factor. (See "Risk"). In the states that use it, it is very powerful, and can mean hundreds of dollars in premium in a single policy term. California is one such state. **The fewer the miles driven, the lower the rate.** If you get too greedy and claim below a certain threshold, <u>you will be asked to verify your claim in order to keep the discount.</u>

This is not too hard to do, but it usually unnecessary if you accurately calculate the miles that you drive. **Most people will overstate their actual mileage driven by thousands of miles, especially young people who see driving huge miles as a badge of honor**, merrily paying higher insurance rates the entire way.

If you do decide that you want this discount, and you need to verify it, free "safety" or "brake check" inspections are available at many shops. **Verification of this discount is typically fulfilled by submitting two documents with odometer readings dated within 30 days of each other**, for example the free "safety inspection," plus a smog check, or an oil change. On the document the shop provides you will be the odometer reading and vehicle identification number, or "VIN" number of your vehicle.

In addition to miles driven, Californians are primarily rated on driving records and claims history, (POI and BI limits are not "technically" used there) **and they are offered two very large discounts in addition to the standard ones:**

"Good Driver" discount is offered when the driver has no more than one violation in the last three years. The discount is as much as 30%, <u>so be sure to take traffic school options when they are offered to you</u>, because having a second violation will increase your rates for up to three years, or until your oldest violation drops off, whichever comes first. Accidents may also involve violations, and could cost you both discounts.

"Safe Driver" is another very large discount, again up to 30%, but it is only offered to those who have no "at-fault" accidents on their records in the last five years. This is one circumstance that you will want to ensure that any claim you submit for damages is not listed as an "at-fault" occurrence unless it actually was. Uninsured Motorist and Comprehensive claims usually do not count against you.

▪**Your strategy here is to make sure that you qualify, (and stay qualified) for both of these discounts, as long as you will be driving in CA**▪

▪Duration of Ownership▪

"Are you the original owner of the vehicle? How long have you owned the car?"

Some states also rate on "duration of ownership" of a particular vehicle. Arizona is one state that uses this factor. <u>As with most discount questions, more is better, and the maximum discount is given for having owned the vehicle for two or more years, with "original" ownership.</u> Obviously if you claim you are the original owner of a 20 year-old car, who just happens to be 18 years old . . . you are probably not going to get this discount.

▪The Marriage Discount▪

"Are you married or single? Divorced or widowed?"

Yes, being a married person is considered a rating factor in calculating auto insurance rates. Perhaps married people get fewer tickets, file fewer claims, or both, who can say, but with most companies in almost every state two married people will pay less on the same policy than two unrelated adults. **That I know of, this discount is seldom if ever verified—the logistics of doing so would be horrifying.**

Nobody has ever told me that they were asked to mail in a marriage certificate or other document, unless perhaps they set up their policy as unmarried, and then tried to switch it after the fact.

Some states allow (or require) that this discount be offered to "domestic partners" whether they are "registered" or not. An agent that you are speaking with may not know of, or care to offer you this discount, so be sure to ask for it if applicable. If needed (and wanted) you could even go down and actually "register" your partnership for a nominal fee at the local courthouse (if domestic partner registration is available in your state).

I believe that this same principle is applied to the other drivers on the policy as well. **Drivers who are "related" to each other (by blood or marriage) in the same household are generally given better rates than those who are not.** "Relatives" or "Children" are rated better than "not related" for example. <u>This claim of relation is not, that I know of, ever verified in any way.</u>

▪Females are usually rated higher (and charged less premium) than males, so if you are a female with a voice that is not distinctly "feminine," be sure to mention that if you are doing a phone quote▪

▪The Claims Free Discount▪

"Have you or anyone in your household filed a claim in the last 5 years?"

The answer may or may not be yes, but if you say "yes," you will definitely not get this discount. Once your reports are run, if nothing is found, this discount will put more money (10% or more) back in your pocket. Not every state offers this discount, but if you get asked this question, either online or by an agent, most likely it is available, and you may qualify for it if you answer the question correctly. **Be careful with this one in conjunction with the Discovery Truth Indicator, or (DSI*), as you may be penalized for not disclosing an accident or claim within the last three years (or however long that particular company rates on occurrences).**

▪Return of Premium Credit▪

Some companies, especially the membership-based ones, will offer an annual or semi-annual "rebate" or "dividend" to you as a reward for safe driving with no claims, or if the company does well as a whole. If you are a high-tiering policy holder with great scoring and maxed-out discounts, (or even if you are not) this may be the last area that you will find the maximum return on your auto insurance premium dollars. **Find a company that both offers you the best rate for your coverage, and a return of premium refund, and you will have found the lowest possible cost auto insurance.**

▪The Multi-Line Discount▪

This may or may not be an actual discount. It is related to the "teaser" discount in that it is meant to retain you as a customer, and keep you from switching to another company, because, the logic goes, it is always easier and cheaper to have all your policies with the same company, correct? The answer is that it *may* be, but this is not always so. **More often than not, the policies that you purchase from one company will be underwritten by another company specializing in that particular product, and therefore it offers better rates and terms.** This is completely logical, but something that is misunderstood by the insurance buying public.

To put it another way, (to my knowledge) the Ford Motor company does not manufacture windshield wipers, yet all of their products are equipped with them, they are sold to you by Ford, and presumably are warranted the same as the other car parts that are actually made by Ford. In this same manner, your car insurance company may offer you a renters or motorcycle policy, and may even offer you a "preferred" or "multi-line" discount for buying them, **but the reality is that you can usually buy these products yourself from the same company at the same price.**

Simply ask, or check into who the policy will actually be "underwritten" by. Is it the same company that the auto policy is with? Usually it is not. In a way, it is like getting something "free" if you buy a product that you probably would not have purchased otherwise. For this kind of discount to matter to you, it must be a *true* savings, for products that you would have purchased anyway, or already have and are shopping their renewal as well.

Otherwise, keep your auto insurance in its own file, and your renters policy, (homeowners, motorcycle, etc) in another, and shop them accordingly, on their own

merits, at each renewal. Over a lifetime of purchasing property and casualty insurance products, <u>this may be your most valuable course of action, and the one that consistently delivers measurable results.</u> You must be willing to invest an hour or two of your time at each policy renewal, or if that is too valuable to waste, have someone else to do the "leg" or "web" work on your behalf. **Remember that a discount is not a discount if it costs you more money than it "saves" you.**

Some companies may offer you additional "credits" for having other lines of business with them, as opposed to "discounts," because discounts are tightly regulated, and credits are much less so. **Whatever the name, the effect is the same, and the result is a lower rate on your auto insurance, in exchange for spending more money elsewhere.**

▪The Future Effective Date▪

This discount is offered as an incentive to get you to buy your policy before you actually need it. That is, buying your policy today with an effective date in the "future" will be cheaper than buying the policy effective today. **It is not always available, and it is often overlooked by both policy holders and agents alike.** If it is offered in your state, it may be as much as 5%. The real trick to this one is that the "future effective date" **can be as early as a few hours or minutes from now!**

Therefore if you do not absolutely "need" your policy to start today (and if you already have coverage for today) check the price if you set the start date in the "future" (tonight at one minute past midnight), and this sweet little discount might surprise you. Of course if you are working with an agent, you could simply ask if the discount is available, or if the price would be different tomorrow than it is today. **Again, the agent may not know about this discount, and if she does, she may not offer it to you for fear that you will not buy your policy today, right now.**

You can pay for and bind the coverage on a specific day, (today) but so long as your policy does not start that same day, you will keep this discount. If you know for a fact that this discount is offered, **make sure that you calendar your policy renewals so that you can always bind your new policy at least a day before you actually need it to start.**

▪The Good Student Discount▪

"Are you in school now? Or have you been in school in the last 12 months? Full time or part-time? Did you (or the driver in question) maintain a 3.0 or better GPA?"

These are the questions asked to determine if you are eligible for this substantial (generally 10%) discount for each driver rating factor that it may apply to. **It is generally only applied to drivers under the age of 25, and it applies to each driver on the policy in that category.** Full time students maintaining a "B" average (3.0) may receive this discount. Many people (and agents!) do not know, however, <u>that it also applies to students who may have left school within the last 12 months, to allow them to continue receiving the discount during the summer months, and during breaks in their education.</u> Like many other discounts, it is seldom if ever verified, although it might be.

Be sure to claim this discount for each driver on the policy if they qualify for it. A "driver training" discount may also be available, (see "<u>Defensive Driver Discount</u>," page 21).

▪The Away At School Discount▪

If your child will be attending school more than 100 miles from your home, <u>and will not have a vehicle with them,</u> you may be able to claim this discount. It is typically around 5%, and will of course only apply if you have the child on the policy in the first place. If you have removed them from the policy because they do not live at home, then there is no premium charge to discount.

▪Level of Education▪

"Are you a high school graduate or equivalent?"

Related to the student discount, this question about "level of education" is asked because (we are told) there is a relationship between the amount of "book learning" a policy-holder may have, and the amount of claims they may potentially file. The less education, the more claims. <u>Perhaps this one is a penalty for simply admitting that you are not a high school graduate or equivalent,</u> **because you will be surcharged in many states if you do admit to this.**

Beyond high school, additional fractional discounts may apply for educational level achieved, from "some college," to "associate degree," "bachelor degree," and finally up to "graduate or doctoral degree." **Where this discount is applicable, more education is always better.**

The "equivalent" of a high school education is precisely difficult to determine. Should a 44 year-old who has been working hard for 25 years at raising his family and paying his taxes qualify as a high school graduate or equivalent? One might even say that this man is a graduate of the "School of Hard Knocks." Of course, having a GED, trade school certificate, or "Proficiency Exam" type certification typically qualifies for this as well.

▪Your strategy here is to carefully determine whether or not you have the "equivalent" of a high school education when you answer this question▪

▪Occupation▪

"What kind of work do you do? Or do you have a degree or certificate in a particular occupation?"

Very few states actually allow this discount; California and Colorado immediately come to mind. **If it applies to you, remember that it is very powerful, as much as 10% or more, so make sure that you answer this question carefully.** <u>The more "technical" or "scientific" your occupation, the higher the discount. Doctors, scientists, and information technology workers will receive the highest discounts (where offered) for "occupation."</u>

Engineers, Craftsmen, and "licensed professionals" also receive high discounts here, (employed or not!) so if you believe you qualify for this discount there is certainly no harm in claiming it. Also, this discount is seldom if ever "verified." <u>Even if you are unemployed, or "not currently working" right now, your degree or certificate in your occupation may qualify you for this discount.</u>

▪However, if you are 18 years old, and claim to be a "medical doctor," do not expect to obtain this discount without verification▪

▪Emergency Roadside Assistance▪

"Do you have AAA, or other roadside assistance?"

I have only seen this discount offered in one state, California. Apparently, those who maintain roadside assistance coverage are better "risks" that will generate fewer claims than those who do not have such a membership. In that state, though, it is a very powerful discount, usually about 10%, so on a $1000 policy this savings will be about $100 per policy term, (six months) or $200 per year, easily exceeding the cost of an actual "AAA" membership.

AAA memberships start at about $60 per year, so if your discount (over 12 months) exceeds this amount, you will be getting cheaper auto insurance, and an AAA membership for nothing, if you claim this discount. It will be verified, usually immediately, so be prepared with your membership number when prompted.

▪Accident Prevention or Defensive Driver training▪

"Have you completed an approved driver improvement course?"

Several states offer this discount in one form or another. Related to it are the "mature driver" improvement course, and the "drug/alcohol awareness" course. **All of these offer some sort of ongoing discount, but most require the submission of the original completion certificate or other verification to actually receive the discount.** NJ and NY, for example, offer similar versions of this discount, and in New York, it is as much as 10% off the liability side of your policy, a substantial amount in those pricy insurance markets.

Additionally, regarding the New York "Accident Prevention" course discount, you will continue to receive the discount for 36 months! This will certainly add up to hundreds, if not thousands, over three years. After three years, simply repeat the class, and keep the discount perpetually. The course is offered online, takes about six hours, and costs about $30!

The actual course requirements and eligibility for each will vary by state, so you will need to first identify which if any is offered, then do a quick online search for the "approved" or "certified" locations that offer it. Many are offered online and can be completed at your own pace. Some may even take motor vehicle and/or insurance underwriting points off of your record. **Either way, if this discount is offered, it is a win for you if you take it.**

▪The PayPal Discount▪

"Do you have, or have you ever started a PayPal account?"

This is a so-called "Affinity Discount" similar to that offered to AAA members. **It is typically about 10%, so if you are asked this question it most likely is available.** If you don't technically have one, you could always start one for free, then your answer would accurately be yes. If you have had one in the past, but "don't remember" your account information, you may still qualify for this discount. It typically applies to all the drivers on the policy, so if any driver has ever had a PayPal account, make sure to claim this discount.

▪The Military Discount▪

"Are you active duty military?"

Louisiana is one state that offers this discount. **It can be as much as 25%, but you must be active duty, or the spouse or dependent of someone who is, to claim it.** If you do, be prepared to provide verification, as it will most likely be requested. **If the discount is not offered to you when you set up your policy, ask for it.** You will need to submit a form, including a copy of your orders/PCS documents, but it will definitely be worth your while to do so. You will not receive the discount until you return the documentation, so act quickly to get the most benefit. Very few states offer this discount, although perhaps more should. **(See "<u>Deployment Exemption</u>" from POI, page 12).**

Members of the military are often required to complete a "driver education" course of one kind or another in order to obtain a permit to operate their personal vehicle on base. They may also have to complete a drug and alcohol course. **If you have completed** either or both of these, be sure to ask if they fulfill the requirement for getting the "defensive driver" and/or "drug and alcohol education" discounts.

▪The Storage Discount▪

If you have a vehicle on your policy that you (or anyone else) will not be operating for a period of time, but you still want to maintain continuous coverage on it, ask your carrier if this discount is available. **You may have to call in and speak to an agent, because even if it is available, it will typically not be something you can select on your insurer's website.** Vehicles that are placed in the "storage condition" may not be driven, must be kept in a "secure location," and will have their liability coverage reduced to the absolute minimum, especially if they are operated on a public road while "stored."

Be very careful with this discount, and do not under any circumstance use it to evade paying legitimate premium. If you do, any subsequent claim may be denied, and you may be assessed additional premium after the fact.

It is a very good option for those who "put up" vehicles for the season, as many folks do in cold climates. Why pay premium as if you were driving the vehicle, when in fact you are not? Stored vehicles will typically retain "comprehensive" coverage, so if the barn collapses, the vehicle is stolen/vandalized, or if a tree falls on it, you will still have physical damage coverage.

"Snowbirds" and others who maintain two residences located at a distance from each other, may find benefit in storing the vehicles in one place while operating those in the other, then reversing the coverages when moving between them. Not all companies offer this discount, so if you live in a cold climate, or maintain multiple residences, look for a carrier that does. The storage discount applies to the stored vehicle only, and may reduce the premium up to 80%.

▪The Paid In Full Discount▪

"Would you like to pay in full for your policy?"

This is your last chance to heavily discount your policy. If available, it will be offered at the point of purchase, and it is very powerful. It will range from 2% to 30% and more, so if it is not offered to you, ask about it. Even if you cannot manage the paid in full option this policy term, knowing how much it will be saving you next term will be your incentive to plan ahead for it.

The cruelly ironic aspect of this discount is that it most often benefits those who least can afford it, the ones with the lowest tiers and highest rates. I have seen drivers who were offered very minimal coverage for over $300 per month, pay as little as $1200 (33% off!) if they pay in full for a six month policy. <u>This discount would of course be in addition to all the other discounts you manage to stack up to the point of actually paying for your policy.</u>

An option usually not offered to you by the insurance company, but frequently available if needed to obtain this large discount is the "third party payment" arrangement. A third party, (not you or your insurance company) makes the payment for you using their method of payment. This person is usually a relative, (Mom or Dad?) or a friend. **They would have to be on the line with you and the agent to give their permission,** and you would then repay them on a private basis.

They would be saving you the amount of the discount by in effect giving you (hopefully) a no or low-interest loan until you repay them. <u>Unused "emergency" credit cards with a 0% interest rate for six months or a year are perfect for this as well.</u> Simply purchase the policy in full with the card, then make six equal payments of the unpaid balance divided by the policy term.

▪Your strategy here is to pay in full at every renewal if possible, and plan ahead to do so▪

◀CHAPTER THREE▶

Coverages

Remember, saving money on your auto insurance coverage isn't just about getting the least amount of coverage for the least amount of premium, **it's about getting the most amount of coverage for the least amount of premium.**

The particular coverages that you are required to carry will vary from state to state, with some very basic similarities. The rule of thumb here is very simply that the more coverage you request or require, the more premium you will pay, subject to the discounts you are eligible for. **If it is explained to you that a coverage is "optional" then you will most certainly pay more premium for your policy if you include this coverage, versus if you "decline" it.**

The most important principle to understand about insurance "coverage" is this:

▪It is a lot like air, in that you will usually not notice or really miss it, until you have none of it▪

The problem here is also that hindsight is always 20/20, as in *after* you have an accident you will realize that you now have a "need" for rental car coverage. Do you have it? You should know these things *before* you realize that you may need them. **Are you calling your insurance company to find out if you have a particular "optional" coverage?** If so, most likely you do not, because when you requested your quote and purchased your policy you specified the "minimum" or "cheapest" possible policy, and this will rarely include any "optional" coverages.

Therefore, **the "best" auto insurance coverage for you is seldom if ever the "cheapest" one,** because the states' "minimum liability" requirement will not do much more for you than ensure that you may legally operate a vehicle on the roads of your state. If you want to know more about your states' specific coverages and the limits of each one, often the best place to start is with a licensed agent.

Ask questions about what coverages are required, and which are optional. Ask for an explanation of any coverage that you do not completely understand. **Do not be afraid to ask for the rate to be recalculated a few times as you price different coverage levels.**

▪When deciding where to spend premium dollars, study the available coverages carefully, then determine the cost of each versus the benefit received▪

▪Bodily Injury (BI)▪

Your state's minimum liability insurance requirement for auto insurance typically will include an amount of coverage for "Bodily Injury" (BI*) to others, that is, the harm you do to other peoples' bodies. It will also include their "lost wages" and other economic damage you may inflict on them, for example. **If you put someone in the hospital for two months, their medical bills will be "X" amount of dollars, but this will not represent the total amount of damage that you will have done to them and their household.**

If they are a high earning individual, (or even if they are not!) you may be liable for the cost of replacing their income, or the price of replacing their service to their household as well. Even a "stay at home" parent, or "domestic engineer" will have their service to their household quantifiable in economic terms. If the injured party must pay to replace that service, then you are responsible for that as well.

What many consumers of auto insurance products do not understand about this coverage is very simply that even though they might "have nothing to lose" right now, (as they often tell me) <u>this may not always be so.</u> So you are in college, and your meals consist entirely of ramen noodles? Your furniture is milk crates and cinder blocks? True enough, no one will want to take those things from you. However, did you plan on going to grad school, maybe law or medical school?

Then you do have something to lose, that is, your *future* earnings. **A smart lawyer will get a judgment for the damages you cause beyond your insurance coverage liability limit,** and you will watch a significant percentage of your earnings go directly from your paycheck to the injured party to satisfy a damage judgment against you, for the next 10 to 20 *years*.

The marginal cost of increasing your BI limit from the "state's minimum" to the next level up, or beyond, is often measured in pennies per day, or a few dollars per month, **and higher levels of coverage may be the best investment you ever make in your lifetime, if you cause serious injury or damage to someone that exceeds your liability**

coverage. The moral of this story is to consider your future as well as your present, when you determine your insurance needs today.

Additionally, carrying high limits of BI is a crucial rating factor when starting your policy, so this limit should already be high, at 100k/300k or better. (See "POI Discount," page 11).

▪Property Damage (PD)▪

Property damage, or PD* is the second liability (to others) coverage that you will be required to carry, and although the amount does vary from state to state, what it actually covers will be the same. **Most often this coverage will pay for the damage you do to the other parties' vehicle, so if you total a brand new Yukon Denali, or a Lexus, your 5k or so in "minimum liability" coverage for property damage will do very little to help you.**

You will be *personally* liable for the other 45k (or more!) damage that you have caused, and again, you will most likely watch your paycheck be garnished for the next 10 or 20 years as you pay off the claim. This awful coverage selection "mistake" is most often made by young people, who think that they have "nothing to lose" or "nothing anyone can take" from them—except their future earnings and lifestyle.

Property Damage also includes the other parties' white picket fence, their sectional sofa, and their 60" big screen TV, if you end up in their living room after an accident, for example. All of those things are property damage. Often overlooked here is damage that you may do to *public* property, such as fire hydrants, utility poles, guardrails, bridge abutments, etc. Rest assured, this kind of damage must also be paid for, and you will be billed for it if you cause it.

PD will pay for this type of damage as well, if you have enough of it. The sad and terrible thing about this particular coverage is that it is very inexpensive (in California, for example, usually four dollars per six months!) to double or quadruple the "minimum" coverage, **and many agents will not offer you this option, for fear that the next company you call or quote with will be a few dollars "cheaper" than they are, and that they will lose the sale.**

Therefore it is *your* responsibility to ask about the price differences between the "minimum" amount of property damage coverage for your state, and an amount that will actually protect you from a "realistic" amount of liability should you actually incur it.

Please do not fall into this "minimum" liability trap, because you do actually get what you pay for.

▪Medical Payments (MP)▪

This is an optional coverage available in many states, and the most important thing to remember about it is this:

It is a First Party benefit, in that it pays for your medical (and other related) expenses due to an occurrence. It will pay up to the limit of coverage for each person in the vehicle, and there is no deductible for using it. Another little known fact about this coverage is that it often includes coverage for you if you are injured as a pedestrian, or while riding a bicycle!

Medical payments (MP) is typically offered in increments from small to large, for example $500 to $10,000. The more coverage, the more premium, but not always proportionately to the increased coverage amount. You may be able to purchase the maximum amount for only slightly more than the minimum. **Even people fortunate enough to have good health insurance, which will in most states pay for these types of injuries, still have to pay deductibles, co-pays, prescription drugs, and other miscellaneous charges not covered by the health policy.**

If this is the case for you, a small amount of MP will do just fine—pick the lowest amount that will cover your expected out of pocket medical expenses should you incur them. **Funeral expenses and ambulance rides also are typically covered by MP**, so drivers who like to live dangerously may want to include this coverage, at an amount large enough to cover the ride to the hospital, a decent funeral, or both, so as to not unnecessarily burden loved ones during their time of loss.

"Extended" Medical Benefits/Payments (EMP) are sometimes offered in addition to the standard coverage. These extended benefits typically offer a death benefit, and sometimes a small amount of income replacement. They may also include a reimbursement for "essential services replacement," which means simply that if you require assistance with common household tasks as a result of your accident-related injuries, you will be compensated up to a designated amount.

Declining these optional coverages has no effect on your premium. $1000 worth of MP can usually be had for about $2 a month (or less!). EMP typically will cost you around another $2 a month.

▪Personal Injury Protection (PIP)▪

This coverage is very much like MP, only with a few key benefits not offered by that coverage. Personal Injury Protection, or "PIP"* as it is usually referred to, may be an optional coverage, or it may be mandatory (in so-called "no-fault" states). **Either way it will protect you for the same things as MP, plus usually a benefit for lost income (wages) suffered as a result of your injuries.** This crucial coverage will help bridge the gap you may have (the "waiting period") between the time when you are first injured, and when your state or company short-term disability income replacement plan kicks in.

If you do not have income replacement now, you may wish to carry the highest (or a very high amount) of MP or PIP, or whatever your budget allows you to afford. If seriously injured, both your injuries and those of your passengers are paid for immediately through this coverage, up to the limit of the policy. If you have the lost wages included, they will also be paid, up to the limit you select per day, week, or year.

Declining this coverage, if it is optional, will decrease the premium you pay. If you live in one of the several mandatory PIP states, you can also reduce your premium for this coverage by choosing a higher deductible, meaning you will pay more out of pocket if you do have an occurrence. **So will your passengers, so be careful when you choose your deductible here.** Some states (Michigan and New Jersey, for example) allow you to select a less expensive "health insurance primary," or "medical only" PIP option, but if you do so, make sure that your health insurance actually covers auto accident -related injuries (**many do not**, including most government-funded health plans like TRICARE, and Medicaid).

"Medical only" PIP means that you will only be compensated for your injuries and related expenses, but not for any lost wages. Of course, if you do not earn an income this may be a good option for you, but if you do, be careful in selecting this coverage just to save a few premium dollars. **It may be something you (and your passengers) will regret.**

Medical Payments and Personal Injury Protection are usually not selectable together, as they largely duplicate each other. Therefore you should choose the one that best suits your particular situation. If you need work loss income replacement, PIP will be the way to go. **If you have no health insurance, higher limits of either would certainly make sense.**

In conjunction with PIP you may be offered a coverage called "Additional Personal Injury Protection," or APIP.* This will offer more coverage for things like lost wages or "income replacement," and is usually offered in increments of so much per day, per week, with more coverage costing more premium. Even at maximum reimbursement, though, the premium for APIP is very low versus the potential return. **Therefore if you are a high income earning individual, this may be especially attractive to you, so be sure to ask for more information about it, as agents will not usually offer or even mention it.**

Guest Personal Injury will extend the level of your PIP to others who have lower limits of PIP from their home state, if any. Again, discuss this coverage with your agent if you feel you might benefit from it, as it is very inexpensive, but if you don't need it, don't spend premium dollar on it.

▪Uninsured/Underinsured Bodily Injury (UMBI)▪

Sometimes offered separately, both of these do essentially the same thing. **They protect you from the physical and economic harm that others do to you, and your passengers.** It is often mistakenly believed (and declined on this basis!) that this coverage protects people who drive around without insurance, (the "uninsured") and "dangit I won't pay one penny for them!" If the other driver is at fault in an accident, and has no or very little BI insurance, UMBI coverage is the one you will want to be carrying.

Some states have made these coverages optional, giving you the right to decline them if you choose to do so. **Because of the very high numbers of uninsured drivers in many states, this coverage is not the cheapest, and is very expensive in some areas.** Be sure to ask about it, because it may not be, relative to your budget. The expense, and whether or not you have health insurance, will be the factors you should consider in making the decision to include or decline this coverage.

This is yet another important reason to carry high limits of BI coverage, at least 100k/300k or more, <u>because the more BI coverage you carry on other people, the more UMBI you can carry on yourself, and your passengers.</u> **You cannot insure yourself for more than you are willing to insure others. Additionally, UMBI will replace your lost wages if you cannot work for a period of time due to your injuries.**

In states with mandatory PIP coverage, though, this coverage would only benefit you after the limit of your personal injury plan had been reached. Florida, for example, requires all drivers to carry 10k in PIP coverage. <u>If you are injured, it does not matter who is at fault or whether they have insurance, until the limit of the available PIP</u>

coverage is reached. Only then would the determination of fault and other liability coverages be looked at to provide additional coverage for you. This usually means your family as well. **Keep this in mind: The limit of UMBI you select, if any, will apply to all the passengers in your car, up the maximum stated amount.**

▪Uninsured/Underinsured Motorist Property Damage▪ (UMPD)

Similar to the UMBI, UMPD pays for the damage to your vehicle, should it be caused by an at-fault driver who has no, (or not enough) PD coverage to pay for your car. However, it makes little sense to carry 100k in UMPD when the vehicle you are insuring is a 1995 Chevy. **Certainly a small amount of this coverage is a great idea, but only up to the value of the most expensive vehicle you own, and will have on your policy.** If that number is $25K, then that is the amount you should pay for. Properly valuing this commonly overlooked coverage could save you $5 or $10 every policy term.

If you will not be carrying collision coverage, then you may wish to seriously consider including UMPD if it is offered. It will have a very low premium in relation to the potential benefit offered.

▪UMPD coverage can be tricky when it comes to one specific area▪

The "phantom vehicle" or "my car hit while parked" claim. The story usually goes like this: "I came out of the supermarket, and discovered that my car had been damaged by someone who then left the scene, leaving no note." Now keep in mind that *some* people will actually cause damage to their vehicle (run it into something), then determine that an "uninsured motorist" or "phantom vehicle" claim would be preferable to an "at-fault collision" claim (and it *usually* is). If you purchase this coverage, make sure you understand the limitations that it may have in this area. The question to ask your agent would be: **"Does this UMPD cover "phantom vehicle" claims?"**

Often agents themselves are unsure about this, and it varies from state to state. If you caused the damage, you should claim it as such. If you did not, make certain that any claim you submit under this coverage is properly listed as a UMPD claim, not an at-fault occurrence. Your wallet will thank you, as at-fault accident claims typically rate against you for three years, and may "tier" against you for five. (See page 31).

Even in states where this coverage is mandatory, you will usually still get to choose the amount of coverage you carry here, and the deductible, (if any). As with BI and UMBI, this amount can be equal to or less than the PD damage you offer to others, for example, if you are insuring other drivers' property for the "minimum liability" of say 5k, then that is all the UMPD you will be able to buy, even if your own vehicle is worth 25k. **Make sure you raise your PD to at least cover the amount of UMPD that you want to buy on your own property, if any.** If your car is worth 2k and the minimum is 5k, then that would then be all the UMPD you need.

"Stacking" of this limit is sometimes offered, and that allows you to multiply the coverage by the number of vehicles on the policy, or in the household. If you live in a one vehicle, one policy household, then "stacking" would most probably be wasted premium dollar spent. Choosing to leave your coverages "unstacked" is often one area where **you can save another few dollars each month, if this coverage is unwanted or needed.**

▪Permissive User/Spousal Liability Enhancement▪

This is an endorsement that you may choose to include with your policy in those states where it is offered. NY and CA are two that I know of. **Where offered, this coverage can be very important, for the following reason.** In CA, for example, your liability coverage for permissive users of your vehicle is typically limited to the state's minimum, or 15k/30k per person for BI, and 5k for PD, per accident. One example where this might apply would be this:

You let your buddy Bob take your new Jetta to the store to get some chips and "supplies" during the big game.

Unfortunately, Bob runs a stop sign, hits a shiny new Mustang GT with your Jetta, and two people in the accident are treated for injuries. Without this enhancement, your coverage for the property damage in this example would be capped at the state minimum of 5k, (and the BI at 15k/30k!) so the remaining 40k in property damage to the Mustang must now be paid by Bob, (or perhaps his insurance company, if any) **and you, because he was driving your car.**

If you have this endorsement, then you would be fully covered <u>if your limits were high enough.</u> **The cost of this coverage is usually less than $10 per policy term, and could possibly be the best spent premium dollars of your entire life.** In NY, the principle is the same, only in this incidence the endorsement applies to your spouse, and is also very affordable versus benefit received. <u>Agents will typically not offer or even mention this coverage, again for fear the next company will not, and they will lose the sale.</u>

▪Emergency Road Service/Towing and Labor▪

If you are offered this coverage, you might consider it if you do not currently have such a coverage through AAA, or some other carrier. Remember that if you are in CA, you should already have purchased road service and would be therefore receiving the discount for it. If you do not have road service, determine the amount of potential return versus the premium dollar charged. Some plans in many states pay only $75 (or less!) per policy term no matter how much it is used. **They may charge you $10-$15 for this, not such a good use of premium dollar, especially when measured against the cost of an actual road service membership.**

▪Comprehensive▪

A good "liability" policy becomes much better by adding this inexpensive physical damage coverage. It will typically cost about 25% or less of the premium for collision coverage on the same vehicle. Comprehensive covers things like fire, theft, vandalism, trees falling on your car, animals jumping out in front of you, hail damage, **basically anything that occurs that damages your vehicle that does not involve you driving it into something**. <u>It will usually be a required coverage on a financed or leased vehicle, at no more than a $1000 deductible.</u>

This is a good "middle-ground" policy to have on nicer vehicles with some good remaining cash value. For example, a ten year-old well kept luxury car or import will be worth a few to several thousand dollars at least, <u>and you could protect yourself very well from those "not at fault" occurrences with very little premium.</u> **$10-$40 per month will buy you this coverage in most states and in most cases, with a very low deductible.**

▪Keep this very important fact in mind when including this coverage in your policy▪

If you run into a object and it is still in the air, it would be normally be covered as a comprehensive claim. <u>If you hit the object after it touches the ground, you are usually</u>

considered "at-fault," and the occurrence is called a "collision." The example of this would be the spare tire flying out of the back of a pickup truck on the highway. **From the time it bounces out of the truck, until the time it touches the ground, it is a "flying object" and any claim submitted would typically be a not-at-fault comprehensive claim.** Once the object hits the ground, running into it will be a collision, or at-fault claim.

Likewise it is with occurrences involving animals. If you hit the animal, or the animal hits you, it is a comprehensive claim. If you swerve to avoid the animal and hit a tree, it is a collision.

▪Collision Coverage▪

This is more physical damage protection for your vehicle. It protects the car specifically against damage that you do to your vehicle. No other drivers are involved, and if they are, they were not at fault, or they were at fault and do not have any insurance. Your PD coverage will pay for the damage you do to their car, but if you are at fault and you do not have collision coverage, you will be essentially "self-insuring" your vehicle for the damage you do to it, or in some cases, that which an uninsured motorist may do.

If the other driver is at fault, and they do not have any PD coverage for your vehicle (or not enough), then this coverage will typically pay for your damages. If you also have UMPD, your deductible would be covered as well, so your out of pocket expense would typically be zero. If you are a safe driver (you have never had any "at-fault" accidents) and your vehicle is nice but older (10 years or more), you may choose to decline this coverage, or carry it with higher deductibles. Collision will most always be a required coverage on a financed or leased vehicle, at no more than a $1000 deductible.

If you decline it, make sure that you understand that you will not be covered for at-fault damage to your vehicle. It is usually the most expensive coverage to have on a policy, so it may not make a lot of sense to pay hundreds or thousands in collision premium to cover a vehicle worth not much more than that! **Remember that all claims are subject to a deductible**, so if you do choose to carry this coverage on an older, lower-valued vehicle, make sure your deductibles are low, say $250 or even $100, to ensure that you get some value returned if you do choose to submit a claim.

▪Remember to check the price of UMPD if you will be declining collision coverage▪

▪Loan/Lease Gap Coverage▪

When you purchase or lease a brand new vehicle, depending on the price and terms, you may be "upside-down" on the contract from the very minute you drive off the dealer's lot. If you wreck the vehicle shortly thereafter, or even a year or two later, it is very possible that you will still owe more on the vehicle than it is worth, "cash value."* This is called the "gap," or difference between what you owe the bank and what they will get from the insurance company. **Even if an uninsured motorist is at fault, you will still be expected to pay off your contract.** This can easily be thousands of dollars, and that is why this coverage is offered.

It will pay up to a stated value above and beyond the cash value of your vehicle, until that loan balance is satisfied. If you know for a fact that your truck is worth 10k, and you owe 12k, then you do have a gap, and could benefit from this coverage, which is usually very inexpensive to carry. If you owe 10k, and the vehicle is worth 12k, then there is no gap, and therefore nothing to cover. Make sure that you understand the exact benefit you are buying, or what exact percentage above the cash value this coverage will offer you.

This is one coverage to watch, because you will not always have a gap on your financed vehicle, and **at the very moment that it provides you no more benefit, you may drop the coverage and reallocate the extra premium elsewhere.** Also, Gap insurance purchased through your insurance company is almost always a better deal than what the dealer will offer you. It will be cheaper on a monthly basis, and can be dropped whenever no longer needed. Gap insurance bought through a dealer will typically be for the life of the contract.

▪Rental Car Reimbursement/Transportation Expense▪

Another often overlooked and sorely missed coverage, when needed. An auto accident is a traumatic experience, and the purpose of insurance is to return you to a state of an equivalent condition to that you were in before you were injured. **If another driver is at**

fault, damages your vehicle, and has adequate coverage, all is well. Your vehicle will be repaired or replaced up to its actual cash value, your deductible for the repair or replacement will be zero, <u>and if you request one you are entitled to a rental vehicle while you wait for repairs or shop for a replacement.</u>

When you will definitely miss this coverage is if you are at fault, or the at-fault driver has no insurance. Now you must pay for your own rental vehicle. Basic rental car coverage is very affordable, but to have this coverage, you must already be carrying comprehensive and collision. **One mistake often made here is to add hundreds of dollars in "full coverage" premium per term to the policy, simply to have a few hundred dollars in rental car reimbursement on a car not worth much more than that.**

▪Accident Forgiveness▪

This coverage may be "earned" or "bought," if and where it is available. Consider it a "get out of accident free" card, as having this coverage typically ensures that if you or any covered operator on your policy has a single "at-fault" accident, you will not be surcharged any additional premium. Accident forgiveness is earned by being with a carrier for a specified period of time, usually five years, and not incurring any losses. Some carriers allow you to "buy" the coverage at any time (of course before you have an accident) for a small fee, usually less than a dollar a month per vehicle on the policy.

Since this is an "optional" coverage, it may show as "declined" on your policy declarations page, so be sure to review your coverages carefully, and to "accept" this coverage, especially if it is free.

Even if it is not "free," it is well worth the small cost, because the surcharge for an at-fault accident ranges from a few to hundreds of dollars per policy term, and this is one surcharge you can easily avoid through this coverage, if available. **Those with young or new drivers on their policy will certainly want this coverage. (See "<u>Youthful Driver Strategies</u>," from page 3).**

Many policy-holders I have spoken with are surprised and upset to discover that they have "declined" accident forgiveness by default. Of course they are very pleased when I can give them the coverage for free.

◀CLAIMS▶

▪Saving money on auto insurance is about making the right decisions at the right time▪

Knowing when and how to file a claim is one area you should be especially careful with, and here is why:

Most physical damage protections will be subject to some kind of "deductible"* which is the amount of money that you will pay out of your pocket before your insurance pays anything on your behalf. The lower this deductible, the higher your premium, because the more risk that you put on your insurance company in the form of lower deductibles, the more risk associated with that policy.

You may choose your coverages with a very low deductible, as low as $50 or even $0, **however my experience has taught me that the lower people carry their deductibles, the more justified they feel in filing claims, their rationalization being "that's what insurance is for!"**

True, that is what insurance is for.

However:

I got a call once from a policy holder who had bought from me a few months ago. **She was a top rated, top-tiered risk, with very good coverage at very little premium.** She had also bought additional insurance products from me. She asked me a very simple question: "I have good comprehensive coverage on my policy, do you think I should file a claim for windshield replacement?" Her deductible was very low.

I did not want to give her my opinion, because it was her policy and her decision, but when you watch someone's rate increase hundreds of dollars in one policy term for one small claim, you get jaded about this question. I suggested that she do not file any claims unless the damages were significant, then offered her a transfer to the claims department. She told me, "uh, no thanks, that's kinda what I had figured, thanks!"

The strategy with any kind of claim that you are considering would be to carefully weigh the cost of making the claim versus any potential benefit. The submission of any claim may cost you your "claims-free discount," and that would be regardless of whose fault the claim was, for the next five years! The point is that even making someone else's company pay you for a small claim may not be in your best interest under every circumstance. Even if you have a "vanishing deductible," (where your deductible drops to zero over time if you do not file any claims), you may still be better off financially to absorb the cost of a small claim, rather than using this benefit unwisely by submitting it for reimbursement. <u>Do the math and decide for yourself.</u>

You will also want to carefully document any insurance company references to the type of claim they are paying on your behalf. Make sure that any "not-at-fault," "uninsured motorist," or "comprehensive" claims are properly recorded as such. These types of claims have a much smaller effect on your rate than would, for example, an at-fault injury accident. <u>Police reports are also crucial in documenting not-at-fault occurrences,</u> the most common examples of which this would be the "phantom driver" or "my car hit while parked" types of claims.

▪If you do submit a claim for a not-at-fault occurrence, make sure to ask your carrier for a "letter of experience," or LOE*, that briefly summarizes the claim and establishes the responsible party▪

For example: "We paid the claim, but our insured was not considered at-fault, because the vehicle was hit while parked." The LOE could be a simple one paragraph email, but be sure to obtain something along these lines from the company that paid the claim, **because the next insurance company you go to may not rate the occurrence against you, if you can provide this documentation.**

◀SUMMARY▶

In Chapter One, we learned about how risk is determined, and some of the strategies to use for boosting your rating tier as high as possible. You should continue this process indefinitely, for example, when your teenage driver grows up and moves out of the home, make sure to adjust your policy accordingly. If you were "roommates," and now you are a "spouse" or "domestic partner," make sure to update that information as well, as soon as that change occurs.

Chapter Two was all about the money you can save by "stacking" as many discounts as possible together. Effectively doing so every policy term will ensure that you have good coverage at an affordable price, so keep checking your eligibility at each renewal, for every possible discount. Often overlooked here are the **"future effective date," "switchover," and "paid in full" discounts.** All three of these are usually available at every renewal, if you shop your coverage well enough.

▪Your strategy to take away from Chapter Two is that first of all, you want to become aware of any and all possible discounts that are allowed and offered in your state▪

Secondly, find a company that offers you favorable underwriting based on your "tier," and also offers as many of the available discounts as possible. **Finally, ensure that you ask for and receive as many discounts as are offered and that you qualify for, each policy term.** There really is no excuse for not receiving the "Accident Prevention" discount offered in NY, for example, yet very few people actually do. A $30, six-hour online class that can save you $100's or $1000's over the next three years? There is no downside to that one.

Coverages was the subject of Chapter Three, and we saw how important it is to carry high limits of bodily injury liability coverage, because not only does that protect you from liability, but it also lowers your rates! People who carry higher limits are seen as better "risks" by their insurance company, and they will therefore tier higher, getting more coverage for the same or even less money.

Saving the most money on auto insurance means spending your premium dollars wisely, and carefully choosing the amounts of each coverage based on cost versus benefit. It also means not submitting minor or frivolous claims unless absolutely necessary, and ensuring that any "not-at-fault" claims are properly reported as such.

Chapter 4 will demonstrate the quoting, rating, and binding process for you, from start to finish. Remember the questions and answers that affect your tiering and discounts, and refer to the appendix whenever you need to, for a quick explanation of some mysterious terminology. <u>Re-read any areas that you have highlighted or noted as particularly relevant to you, before you quote your new policy.</u>

◄CHAPTER FOUR►

Sample Quote Process

You have studied this guide, (or at least glanced through it, and saw that you could skip to this point) **and now you are ready to quote and bind your coverage.** For our purpose here I will assume that you have called in to speak to an agent. The questions, and the process will be much the same if you go online to purchase your policy, although the order in which they are asked may vary slightly. Questions that affect rate tier and discount are highlighted and explained in parenthesis. **Not every question will be asked in every state, but you can be assured that if you are asked about something, most likely there is a discount or rating factor associated with the answer.**

Most of the questions will be asked about the Primary Named Insured, or PNI, and that is always the first person listed on the policy. The Credit-Based Insurance Score, or CBIS, will be applied to the PNI in most states, so you should have already determined which driver has the best score, and that is the person who should be on the phone with the agent, or online. Some discount factors do apply to the additional drivers on the policy, **so if you are asked about them, keep the answers in mind that will generate the highest discount.**

You and the agent are on the phone:

Agent: "Hello, thanks for calling Megasurecorp! My name is John. How can I help you?"

You: "I'm calling to get an auto insurance quote."

Agent: "Great! What I will do is ask you some questions about you as a driver, and your driving records, then we will get you the best rate we can, ok?

Agent: "We can start with your name. **And what is your garaging address and zip code please?"** (Tiering for risk is already starting. Remember to quote from prospective zip codes you may be moving to. One home or apartment across the street from another may be 30% less).

Agent: "Also, do you own your home, rent, or live with your parents?" ("Homeowners" are given a discount, "renters" are not)."

Agent: "**And, do you have any auto insurance now? How long have you had insurance, and how much of it do you carry?**" (POI tiering is being applied. <u>Make sure to have at least one day of POI with limits of 100k/300k, before you quote your policy.</u> The longer you have POI, the better the discount, up to six years. Only the first six months or year is typically verified. <u>Also, having POI will get you the "switchover" discount, if offered</u>).

Agent: "**Can you verify your POI?**"

You: "Of course."

Agent: "Good! Now I will read you a disclosure regarding the use of credit-based insurance scoring. **What is your Social Security Number?**" (CBIS tiering is being applied. <u>The driver with the highest score should always be the PNI</u>).

Agent: "And now some questions about you as a driver. **Are you married, single, divorced, or widowed?**" (<u>Married and Widowed receive discounts, "Domestic Partners" may also receive the discount, registered or not</u>).

Agent: "**How old were you when you got your driver's license in the U.S?**" (Driver experience factor is being applied. <u>The more years of U.S. or sometimes Canadian operating experience, the better the discount</u>).

Agent: "**What is your highest educational level achieved? Are you a high-school graduate or equivalent?**" (<u>"Less than high school" will be surcharged. Anything beyond "high school equivalent" may have additional fractional discounts</u>).

Agent: "**What is your occupation? Or, what kind of work do you do?**" (<u>Science, medical, technical, and IT type fields receive the highest discount here</u>. Being "certified" or licensed would qualify, even if you are "not currently working." It may also be asked about your spouse or domestic partner).

Agent: "**Do you have AAA or other road service assistance?**" (<u>CA drivers receive a 10% discount for having AAA.</u> You will be asked to verify immediately).

If you (or any driver on the policy) is under 25 years old:

Agent: "**Are you in school now? Or have you been in school in the last 12 months? Full-time? Did you maintain a "B" average or better? (3.0)**" (<u>Full-time students under the age of 25 typically receive this discount of about 10%. This is seldom if ever verified</u>).

Agent: "Let's talk about your driving records. Do you have any accidents, violations, or claims in the last three years? Do you have any major violations in the last five years?" (You should already know the driving and accident records of all the drivers you are quoting for, so that you will not be penalized for the Discovery Truth Indicator, or DSI. You should also ask how long this company rates on what types of violations).

Agent: "Now some questions about the vehicle. Will you be using it for any business or commercial purpose?" (Business use is surcharged at the very least. Commercial use will DNQ you immediately with most carriers).

Agent: "Would anyone else but you drive the vehicle? Are there any other drivers in your household? Are they relatives or roommates?" (If there are, and they have their own vehicles and insurance, then you do not have to insure them. Or you may simply exclude them from your policy).

Agent: "How many miles per day/week/year will you be driving the vehicles?" (the more miles driven, the more risk, and therefore higher premiums). Anything at, or just under 7500 miles is usually merely self-reported. Claims of extremely low miles driven annually will most likely have to be verified).

Agent: "How long have you owned the vehicle? Are you the original owner?" (The longer the period of ownership, the better the discount. "Original ownership" receives the highest discount).

Agent: "Will you be commuting to NY or NJ?" (Commuting to a job will be surcharged. Merely driving into those states to visit is not "commuting").

Agent: "Does the vehicle have an alarm or satellite-based theft deterrent system?" (Any vehicle with "keyless entry" also has an alarm, and most GM vehicles have On Star. Activated or not, it still qualifies. This is used to discount comprehensive coverage).

Agent: "Do you have a PayPal account?" (Some companies will offer you an "affinity" discount simply for having a PayPal account, or having had one at some time in the past. This can be as much as 10% off).

Agent: "Have you completed a defensive driver, accident prevention, or mature driver course? (These are often available online, and cost very little. The discount ranges from 2% to 10%).

Agent: "Now let's talk a little about coverages. What coverages would you like to carry on your vehicle?"

At this point, all of your underwriting, tiering, and rating factors have been applied. You will then select the coverages that are important to you, and you are now ready to "bind" your coverage. You do that by paying for the deposit, or the total policy in full. **(Remember the "paid in full," and "future effective date discounts?" Now is the time to grab them).**

Once you provide a method of payment, typically the agent or program will immediately notify you of what additional "verifications" are needed. <u>Often your driving records, claims history, and POI will verify instantly.</u> If not, make sure to follow up on any verifications that are requested within the specified time frame, **and be prepared to lose any discount that you claimed but could not verify.**

◀AFTERWORD▶

The reason I know these ten questions so well, is because I have asked them ten thousand times. I want to thank Marshall Mathers, whose own courageous work inspired me to write this guide.

Hearing and seeing the "wrong" answers to those questions costing people millions of dollars, also has greatly motivated me.

Tell your friends and family about how you have benefited from this Guide. Lend them your ebook. They will thank you for it! **If you don't have the ebook version, get one, because you will always be entitled to the most current version, free of charge.**

Remember to "brush up" on your situation and the available discounts at each policy renewal, **especially if you have moved to another town or state.**

Always consider your insurance needs right here and now, not as they were when you set up your policy years ago. I have seen millionaires with "minimum" liability auto insurance policies. Like the Constitution, your insurance contract is a living document, meant to be changed and evolved along with you and your family.

Honest and fair reviews are always welcome. Your opinion counts.

▪Suggestions for topics to include in future versions of *Ten Questions* can be sent to the author directly▪

johndavidauthor@yahoo.com

▪Advanced Topics▪

This section is for advanced or experienced insurance consumers and agents. Here you will find some special topics and state-specific coverages. Again, most folks will not find this information useful until they have mastered the rest of this guide.

ID Cards: People are often concerned by whose name appears on their insurance ID card, the one they carry around in their glove box or wallet.

▪An important concept to remember about auto insurance coverage is simply this▪

Insurance follows the car, not the driver; therefore it is immaterial who is driving the car when the request to produce insurance information is made. **Santa Claus could be driving your car, get pulled over, and as long as the car is insured, so is good Saint Nick.** Many people find comfort in seeing their name on the insurance card, however, and I see no reason why you or your agent should not produce one with whatever names you wish on it. Young drivers, newly licensed, are particularly happy to see their name on the insurance card, sort of a "rite of passage," I guess.

Most state insurance ID cards only have room for two names, with the default name/s usually the registered owner/s of the vehicle, or the named insured on the policy. Typically the second name is selectable from a drop-down menu, and here is where you will find the names of the other operators on the policy. Simply select the names you want to appear on the card, print them out, and repeat the process as many times as necessary in order to produce cards with everyone's name on them. Again, this is not needed, except perhaps in jurisdictions with less informed law-enforcement officials. **In those locations, of course you will want to provide whatever the officer has told you is "required."**

In states where only the "registered" owner/s names will appear by default on ID cards, (and this option may not be changed) simply update the name of the secondary or joint registered owner to that which you want to appear on the card, then change it back to the "actual" name when you have finished printing the card.

▪Umbrella Policies▪

An "umbrella" policy is used to increase the overall limits of liability coverage you have, beyond the limits of your auto, homeowners, and possibly commercial liability policies. People with significant income or assets, or both, should definitely consider obtaining this type of policy. **Households that have recently increased their liability exposure tremendously, by adding a youthful or "new" driver, should also seriously consider an umbrella.** (See "Youthful Driver Strategies" from page three). The cost of an umbrella is usually between $20 and $50 per month for the first million of coverage, and that limit can be extended to a theoretically unlimited amount. Of course, the more coverage, the more premium.

In certain circumstances, people with few assets and low incomes, but high potential future incomes, may also be well-served by an umbrella policy. One example of this would be a surgical intern, just out of school. That person's potential income is what needs to be protected. (See "Bodily Injury" from page 26).

Consult a trusted financial advisor or attorney for more information about your liability exposure versus your coverage. The rule of thumb might be simply this:

▪**If you think you need an umbrella policy, you probably do. Like a mint, if someone offers you one, you probably should take it**▪

▪**"No-Fault" States and Coverages**▪

Keep this in mind. **There is no such thing as a true "no-fault" state, in the purest definition of the word.** If possible, a determination of fault will always be made, to ensure that the responsible party is held accountable for the injuries and damages that they cause. I have had people actually tell me that "I don't need more than the state minimum property damage and bodily injury coverage, because this is a no-fault state, and the other guy's insurance has to pay for him and his car."

Really? That statement could not be more incorrect, but there is enough truth in it to confuse people, which is why that belief is so dangerous. If it were absolutely true, a driver could "bumper-car" their way merrily down the street, damaging every vehicle they encounter with no civil liability, although perhaps criminal charges would be filed.

What "no-fault" coverage typically applies to is the bodily injury and lost wages incurred by the occupants of each vehicle, meaning that they would submit a claim for damages to the insurance company that is ensuring each respective vehicle, without regard to a determination of liability. **Those injuries and damages would be paid for up to the limits of the "no-fault" coverage for that state. (See PIP, from page 29).**

However, once that coverage is exhausted, the determination of fault will definitely come into play, and the responsible party will have to pay for the damages they have caused, under the BI and PD limits of their policy. **Ideally they will have enough of each.**

▪New Jersey▪

"Full versus Limited Tort" options: A "Tort" in a nutshell is a harm or wrong that has been done to you that results in economic, physical, or emotional damage. New Jersey allows you to select either full or limited tort on your auto insurance policy. **"Full Tort" means that you retain the option to sue for "emotional distress" and other typically non-monetarily quantifiable damages.** "Limited Tort" means that you may still sue the other party for damages, but only for things that you can actually produce a receipt for, as in: my medical bills were "X" dollars, my lost wages were "Y" dollars, therefore I am suing you for "Z" dollars.

An example of a "Full" Tort claim would be: "Because of the accident that you caused, my face was disfigured by this scar, then my girlfriend left me because of the scar, and my heart was then broken by her leaving me. Therefore you owe me one million dollars for my broken heart." How much is a broken heart worth? That is something for the lawyers and the courts to decide, and if you have full tort coverage you retain the right to have that value decided in court. Lawyers absolutely love full tort, insurance companies not so much, **which is why they will charge you substantially more premium for full versus limited tort coverage.**

▪A LITTLE KNOWN FACT ABOUT LIMITED TORT▪

If you are disfigured or permanently disabled by a negligent party, or have suffered "grievous harm," you may still sue for non-monetary damages, even under the limited tort option. If you make your living with your good looks, or have other special situations to consider, you may wish to pay the extra premium associated with full-tort coverage. **Most people are well-served with the limited option. Consult your attorney if you are unclear about which option best suits your particular circumstances.**

▪State Specific Information▪

This is not intended to be all-inclusive by any means, **since insurance requirements are constantly changing**, and are different from state to state, as discussed in the introduction to this guide. Because something is not listed here does not mean that it does not exist, of course. With that said, here are some interesting state coverages.

▪Michigan▪

"Broad-form," versus "standard" and "limited" collision coverage. What does this all mean? Essentially, it is allowing you the ability to "insure your deductible" for collision coverage, by adding a "determination of fault" to the mix. Of course each of these has a different premium associated with it, but understanding those differences is crucial to getting the most out of your premium dollar. Most insurance agents and online providers will default you to the broad-form coverage, unsurprisingly the most expensive option.

Agents will tell you "it's the best coverage!"

Is it?

The answer is it may be, but not always. Here is what each one means, in a nutshell. **"Broad-form" simply means that no matter what or who causes the collision damage to your property, you will have coverage, and you will not pay a deductible if you are less than 50% at fault.** "Standard" means that no matter who is at fault, you will have coverage, and you will always pay your own deductible. "Limited" means that if the occurrence is with another auto, and is determined to be your fault, you will not have any collision coverage at all!

Obviously the limited option, (the least expensive) is nearly useless in all but a few instances, which is why financed vehicles may not carry this option, as it is unacceptable to most finance companies. While there may be circumstances where it does apply, most any vehicle that you would carry collision coverage on will certainly be worthy of at least the standard version.

In nearly every circumstance I have seen, the standard collision option is the perfect balance between premium cost and benefit received. Simply compare the cost difference between broad and standard, because the difference in premium is what you are paying to insure your deductible. A higher deductible at a lower cost may make sense under the broad form, because if you are a safe driver, you will not be paying it anyway. Conversely, why pay extra premium for the broad form option, when your deductible is $100?

The take-away from this is to "do the math" between the broad and standard options, remembering to consider your deductibles, and make the best choice for you regarding cost versus benefit. Often the standard coverage is the better option, when looked at realistically. Your agent may resist this choice, (remember she gets paid commission based on the premium you pay, more premium = more commission) and may even offer you the old "what-if?" hypothetical to convince you that the more expensive option is always better.

▪California▪

In addition to the permissive user liability endorsement that you should already have on your policy (see "Coverages" from page 32) UMPD has a two-fold function in the Golden State. If you choose not to carry Collision coverage, it will pay up to $3500 if an uninsured motorist destroys or damages your car, subject to a small deductible. This is a great coverage to have on an older vehicle with good cash value, as it is very affordable. **If you do carry Collision, you can also choose UMPD, but it will show up on your policy as "waiver of collision deductible."**

This means that if your vehicle is damaged by an uninsured motorist, your out-of-pocket expense will be zero, so if you are a safe driver (few or no at-fault accidents, ever) you are more likely to be hit by another driver than you are to cause an accident yourself, and CA has literally millions of uninsured drivers. In any case, UMPD delivers great value for the few premium dollars it will cost you.

CA will also rate DUI convictions against you for 10 years, (from any state) so do not expect to receive the "good driver" discount if you have such convictions. If you were looking for excuses to move out of the state anyway, add this to your list, as nearly every other state will only rate DUI convictions for five years, or less.

▪Georgia▪

UMBI coverage here may be selected as "added to" or "reduced by" at-fault liability limits. By default your policy will show the more expensive "added to" limit. You may select (by endorsement) the "reduced by" option, but remember that if you do so, whatever coverage you have will be reduced by the amount of at-fault liability payable under the other parties' insurance. If both of you are carrying "minimum liability," then the "reduced by" option is effectively useless. **If you will be carrying UMBI, then the extra benefit of "added to" coverage is certainly worth the small cost.**

◀APPENDIX▶

TO

TEN QUESTIONS

This material is organized alphabetically. For further clarification, chapter references are also included where necessary.

▪100k/300k▪

This means "100 thousand dollars per person, 300 thousand dollars per accident." This is the "Sweet Spot" for prior insurance coverage tiering (POI). It will usually result in the maximum amount of discount obtainable, and it is the minimum amount of liability coverage that should be carried.

▪Additional Personal Injury Protection (APIP)▪

Usually an optional coverage, this will offer you more coverage for lost wages and other services. The additional premium for this coverage is very small, so be sure to ask about it. You may choose the amount of coverage to carry.

▪Base Rate▪

The starting point for determining the amount of premium you will ultimately pay. Different "tiers" will have different base rates, and your discounts will come off of this amount. Your goal here is to tier as high as possible, then discount that tier by stacking as many discounts as possible.

▪Bind▪

To bind your policy means to secure an insurance contract at an agreed upon price, for a designated period of time, typically six months. After the "underwriting period" typically no longer than two months or sixty days, your rate is guaranteed with very few exceptions, such as the revocation of your license.

▪Bodily Injury (BI)▪

This is the first of the liability coverages that will be required in nearly every state. It is usually expressed as two numbers, separated by a slash, as in 10k/20k, 25k/50k, etc. This is the amount in thousands of coverage per person/per accident that you will have to protect you from liability. **It is a tiering factor for POI, and the maximum tier is usually achieved when you carry 100k/300k.** You are personally responsible for the damage you cause in excess of your liability insurance.

▪Cancellation▪

When you contact your insurance carrier, or they contact you, any time before the end of your current policy term, and request that the policy be terminated. Technically this could be one day into the policy, or one day from the end of the policy. If applicable and allowed, your carrier may charge you a fee if you initiate the cancellation. If you are unsure about the fee, simply contact them and ask, or always "non-renew" your policies, and you will never be charged this fee.

▪Cash Value▪

This is the actual or market value of the vehicle, sometimes called the book value. It may or may not be equal to the loan balance. Make sure you know your vehicle's cash value, and your deductible as well. You may want to get a second opinion if you and your adjuster disagree on this value.

▪Credit Based Insurance Score (CBIS)▪

The CBIS is used to tier you for risk, and is loosely based on your credit or "FICO" score. On a multi-driver policy, your strategy here is to determine the person with the highest CBIS, and ensure that they are the PNI on the policy.

▪Deductible▪

The amount of money that you pay out of your pocket, before your insurance company pays any claim on your behalf. The lower this amount, the higher your premiums will be, and the higher your deductible, the lower your premiums will be. Most finance companies will not accept a deductible over $1000, and extremely high deductibles are effectively useless in many situations.

▪Discovery Truth Indicator (DSI)▪

This is a re-tiering that is applied to you if information is found on the underwriting reports that contradicts what you have disclosed. In other words, failure to disclose accidents and violations will result in higher premiums when the occurrences are "discovered" during the underwriting process. Your strategy here is to avoid this at all costs by obtaining a copy of your MVR and accident history before you quote your policy.

▪Does Not Qualify (DNQ)▪

Does not qualify means that the agent or program has determined, either through the responses you have provided, or the reports that have actually run, that you are ineligible for that particular companies underwriting requirements. Disclosing a commercial use, for example, will instantly disqualify you with many companies, as will a DUI, or even simply having no prior insurance in some markets, such as New York. Too many accidents or motor vehicle points will also DNQ you with many underwriters.

▪Flat Or "Named" Driver Exclusion (NDE)▪

A simplified exclusion process whereby you list the drivers you do not want to cover on your policy by name and date of birth, pay the requisite fee, if any, and are no longer required to insure them. **Of course, excluded drivers are not covered under your policy if they cause an occurrence while driving your vehicle.** California is the most populated state offering this option.

▪Letter Of Experience (LOE)▪

This can be as simple as a one paragraph email from your carrier at the time of the occurrence. It would state the date of the occurrence, the amount of the claim, and whether any determination of fault was made. Ask for one of these for any claim you submit that is not an at-fault. Police reports are also used as supporting documentation, so if possible be sure to get one.

▪Motor Vehicle Report (MVR)▪

Sometimes called an abstract, this is the report that you would get before you quote your auto insurance. Knowing exactly what is on your report will ensure that you are not charged for any DSI penalties. This would apply to all the drivers on the policy.

▪Non-renewal▪

If you know that you will be changing carriers soon, you should contact your existing company and inform them that you will be ending your contract at the end of the current term. Make sure the dates are exactly clear to avoid any cancellation fee. For example, if your policy term runs from 1/1 to 7/1, ending your policy on 6/30 would be a cancellation, but non-renewing your policy on 7/1 would not.

▪Occurrences▪

An occurrence or "accident" is an event that results in a claim for liability payment from one party to another, usually the policy holder and the insurance company. Some occurrences are rated differently than others. Your strategy here is to ensure that any a claim you do make is properly reported if it is a "not at fault," or "comprehensive" claim. At-fault occurrences nearly always lower your tier, thereby increasing your rate. (See LOE in "claims").

▪Personal Injury Protection (PIP)▪

PIP may be a mandatory or an optional coverage. In either case, you will have the option to select how much of this coverage to carry, your deductible, or both. PIP deductibles should be kept as low as possible within budget, and coverage limits should be higher if you have no health insurance of your own.

▪POI▪

This is your prior auto liability insurance history, or "proof of insurance," and it is a strong tiering factor. **The more coverage, (up to 100k/300k) and the longer you have had it (up to six years) the better the discount.** Typically only the first six months or year of POI will be verified. Being a "named insured" on someone else's policy, even for one day, will still qualify. Canadian insurance may qualify, as some "company car" type policies. Foreign and commercial insurance do not qualify.

▪Primary Named Insured (PNI)▪

The primary named insured is the first person listed on the auto insurance policy, and is the person primarily used to tier the policy for risk. Credit based insurance scoring only factors on the PNI, even if there are four drivers on the policy. Making sure that the person with the highest tier is always first on the policy is the best strategy here.

▪Property Damage (PD)▪

This is the second liability coverage required in most states. It will pay for the amount of damage you do to the property of others, and is available in limits as low as $5k. 25k is the minimum amount of PD that should be carried in any state, with 50k or 100k preferable. The price difference between "states minimum" coverage and those higher limits is sometimes only pennies per month. You are personally liable for any damage you cause in excess of this limit.

▪Surcharged▪

This means that you will pay an additional amount of premium in addition to your base rate, because you represent additional liability to the underwriter. Business use is almost always surcharged, as is commuting into New York or New Jersey from adjacent states. Your strategy here is to avoid as many surcharges as legitimately possible.

▪Tiering▪

This is the process of rating you for the amount of underwriting risk you are seen to represent to the insurance company. Many factors affect risk tiering, and your goal is to start your policy at the highest possible tier, then "re-tier" higher over time as your risk factors improve (credit score gets higher, etc).

▪Verification▪

This is the process of providing documentation in support of a particular discount or tiering factor. Many verifications are instantly obtained electronically, such as your driving records and claims history. In some cases, your POI will be electronically verified as well. If you are asked to verify something, make sure you understand what is needed. Remember to submit exactly what is requested within the time frame specified. If you do not, prepare to have the unverified discount removed.

10071914R0004

Made in the USA
Charleston, SC
04 November 2011